Making it at Uni

Making it at Uni

Sally Bartholomew   Jodi Withers

Illustrated by Phil Guest

For

Barrie, Emma, James, Joe and Lily

Paul

Contents

ACKNOWLEDGMENTS

We are grateful to the following people who have supported us in the writing of this book:

Cherry, for her attention to detail in proofreading our drafts.

Phil, for his wonderful illustrations – they really made us smile.

Adam, for all of his inspiring and helpful words.

Our colleagues, who have been so encouraging, and who have endured our obsession with this book over the last few months.

To our families, who continue to humour us!

And finally, thank you to all of our past and present students, from whom we have learnt so much.

1 DECISIONS

About this book

This book is written for students who are thinking about going to university and for those who have just begun their journey at university. You may be deciding whether university is for you or you might be nervous about taking the first few steps into higher education.

We wrote this book to help you navigate your way through the challenges of the first year of your degree. It will give you an insight into the realities of studying as a student, share tips and advice and (hopefully) entertain you by sharing the stories of other students. It aims to be a relationship counsellor, academic skills tutor, motivator, and agony aunt – a hand to hold, a shoulder to cry on – and it promises to make you laugh through possible university-related tears.

Don't take this book too seriously. This is not a text book. This is a 'help' book; a book to help you on the journey to becoming a student in higher education. You are in charge of your life – 'Making it at Uni' is not in charge of your life. Find a way of making this book work for you. We have included a few blank pages for your notes at the end of the book, but if you feel that you need more space then staple some extra bits of paper onto the pages. Only read this book with a pen in your hand – this is your book, write on it and make it your own. Draw smiley faces beside the points which you think will suit you or cross out bits that you think you can manage without. Fill in the tables and have a go at the exercises, share these ideas with your fellow students on social media – if something's helped you, then it may be that it will help another student.

Some students never 'solve the puzzle' of university, and so they don't get the most out of their experience. In the most extreme cases, students drop out because they don't understand how it all works. Therefore, our first piece of advice to you is to be proactive. Don't wait and expect help to be forthcoming. It is much better to seek it out for yourself. There is lots of help if you know where to look.

Many lecturers and administrative staff have forgotten what it is like to be new to university study, so they might make lots of assumptions about what you know or need to know. This means that they might not explain what they consider to be common knowledge. In fact, a lot of the time this stuff is not obvious at all. You will have to make it your business to find out what's what. This book will help you with this.

We never say that the journey into higher education is going to be an easy one, but with the help and advice from this book it is our hope that students and prospective students find the transition of going to university a little less tricky; a little warmer – more comfortable and joyful than diving into it cold! This may all sound daunting, but after reading this book, you will have a sense of how life will be at university, and you will have a good idea of the steps you can to take to make a flying start.

You will have lots of questions. Here are some of the questions that are probably swirling around your mind as we speak:

Am I doing the right thing?

Well, only you can answer that! But the opportunity to learn new stuff, gain higher qualifications, grow in confidence, and prove you can succeed, is reason enough to go for it.

Am I up to this? I'm not clever enough!

Well, having read this far, you will not be surprised to hear that we would argue that yes, you are up to it and you can succeed. How do we know? Well, for a start, you are reading this book. That shows that you want to succeed, and the desire to succeed is more than half the battle. Forget notions of 'intelligence' and 'cleverness' – perseverance and determination count for so much more. The cleverest person in the world will not succeed without them, so that shows you just how far being 'clever' gets you.

'Going to university is a great idea!'

I'm a mature student – is it going to be OK?

These days, universities welcome mature students with open arms, offering alternative entry requirements and foundation years to encourage mature students to apply. According to statistics, in 2017, 591,000 mature students started a degree course[1], so it is likely that you will be one of many mature students on your course. In some universities, mature students even make up the majority of the student body: the Open University, for example. There are loads of examples of older students to inspire you – for example, in 2017 the BBC reported on a student who started a law degree at the age of 79![2]

So, who cares what your age is? You shouldn't care, and you will find that your fellow students won't, either – they will probably be more concerned about themselves and will possibly look to you for guidance and support!

I'm a distance/part-time student – will this book help me?

Although this book will focus on some issues that may be specific to studying at a 'brick' university, there is a lot here that you will find useful and will relate to as a distance and/or part-time student. For example, you won't be able to drop into your tutor's office in person, but you may be able to have virtual meetings, and you will still need to know how you might go about creating a productive studying environment and building a rapport with your fellow students.

---

[1] Higher Education Statistics Agency

[2] http://www.bbc.co.uk/news/education-41573213

How to use this book

Just like reading other academic books, there is really no need to read this book from cover to cover, although you can if you like! Feel free to dip in and out of the chapters that grab your attention, when it is useful for you to do so.

We will be explaining stuff like: *what's the difference between a lecture and a seminar?; what is a 'semester'?; what am I supposed to do with all of this free time?; how will I cope with meeting new people?; what do I need to know about budgeting my money?; how do I reference the book I have read and used to write my essay?*

As you will go on to see, there is a fairly equal balance between how to study effectively (the second half of the book) and the other aspects of university life such as making friends and generally what to expect from your new life (the first half).

Why should I take your advice?

Rule number one in deciding whether a book is worth reading: find out what the authors' credentials are. Here are ours:

We both work in a university where our roles are very much focused on supporting students during the first weeks and months of their degree. Each student we have met has helped to form the advice which we put forward in this book. No two students are the same, you are not the same as your friend, but there is certain underpinning advice that both you and your friend can benefit from; that advice is what you will find in this book.

Also, we are both still students ourselves, as we are both studying for our PhDs alongside our 'day jobs'. So, we do know how daunting starting a new course at a higher educational level can be.

To be honest, though, we're fascinated by the whole process of students joining their new academic community. Every September we welcome a new bunch of students and accompany them on the rollercoaster ride that is their first year. And we say rollercoaster ride, because it really is one – nobody, we repeat, nobody has a completely smooth ride. And that's as it should be – nothing worth doing is ever easy, right? There will be lots of ups and downs. But we really hope you have the time of your life, and that this book helps to smooth out the bumps a little.

We would love to hear your stories about your first year at university. If you'd like to share your experiences, suggest some tips for future students, comment on this book or just say hello, feel free to email us at **makingitatuni@gmail.com**, visit our blog at **makingitatuni.wordpress.com**, or follow us on Twitter **@makingitatuni**.

Good luck!

2 EXPECTATIONS

First of all, well done: if you're reading this book then you are either thinking of going to university or may already be getting on with your studies in higher education - congratulations! But the world of higher education (for that is where you are now) is somewhat different from where you may have been before. Here are a few things that, over the years, new students have pointed out to us as the main differences between what they have been doing before, and their first taste of university life.

I have to be self-motivated

You will find that you will be attending lectures (or missing lectures because you overslept!) where your lecturer 'talks at' you for a period of time. You will probably not find this the best environment to learn – how can this possibly work? It does. It goes without saying that you need to attend ALL sessions available to you. Keep motivated; the more you attend, the more motivated you will become. Most of the time lectures will be accompanied by a 'seminar'. A seminar is usually a smaller group of students who discuss the ideas presented in the lecture. The seminar may be the place where you can ask questions, clarify anything that you found confusing in the lecture, learn from your fellow students and think more deeply about your subject.

You may be given reading to do for the next lecture; always have a bash at the reading even if you don't fully understand what it's on about. The reading you are given for the lecture will certainly help you – so read it! Reading is such an essential part of university life that we have included a chapter (Chapter 7) to guide you in your reading.

You will find that you have a lot of *free time*. You won't be at university from 9am-5pm every day, like college or work. So, what are you going to do with your *free time*? You might not be set weekly deadlines for work to be handed in at university, but this does not mean that you don't have anything to do; you will have to set your own mini-deadlines and work out your own routine of getting things done. Your lecturer will expect you to pop off to the library and read about the topic he/she has been talking about. You must be motivated enough to do this, for example, no-one is going to remind you about deadlines, no-one is going to set your alarm for you to get up, no-one is going to force you to walk over to the library. *Spend* time, don't *waste* it.

It may be that you are already a very self-motivated person and so you won't have problems in organising yourself: if so, brilliant, you can skip the next bit. But, if you have any doubts that you are an organisation superhero, then try out the task below:

When you know them, fill out the table below with the times of your lectures for the first semester then think about how you are going to spend your *free time*: remember, spend time, don't waste it.

	Time in lectures	Free time and how I am going to spend it (not waste it)
Mon		
Tues		
Wed		
Thurs		
Fri		

It looks a bit more serious when you write it down, doesn't it? For the first few weeks use this table to motivate yourself in order to use your free time wisely - after which, go it alone. You *can* do it.

I was surprised at how big the classes were; sometimes it was a bit scary

You may be lucky enough to be on a course with a small number of students, but it is more common to have to sit in a lecture theatre with 200 other students. So, get ready, and don't be shocked. Make sure you say hello to the students around. And smile! Smiling makes you relax and seem friendly. Lecture theatres are scary places. They can be scary places for teachers and lecturers too! So you're not on your own. Make sure you are equipped and that you bring along some paper and a couple of pens. Lots of students benefit from writing in different colours, so buy at least four different coloured pens and see how this works for you. Although sitting in a very busy lecture may not be the time to ask loads of questions, remember that you have the seminars and group tutorials for these questions. Make sure you make notes in your different coloured pens of the questions that you need to ask. Your lecturers are the perfect people to answer your questions regarding your work. Do you know the full name of your lecturer? Do you know their email address? Do you know when they have set aside time to see you about your work? If the answer is not 'yes' to all of these questions, then make sure that you find out. We talk further about getting the most out of your lecturers in Chapter 3.

Lectures may be very busy places, but you will always have the opportunity to sit down with a subject specialist to discuss things that you are not clear on. Every lecturer has time in their timetable where they must be available to speak to their students. This time is often called *office hours*. Find out when your lecturers have their office hours and note down the information about your lecturers below, for future reference:

Module	Lecturer	Email	Office hours

I find deadlines petrifying

You will find that you will have deadline dates to hand in any work that has to be assessed on your course. These are important dates. Make a note of them and don't forget them. They are usually not flexible and the excuse that you didn't have the right date written down just will not wash. Try hard to manage your workload way, way before the deadline. This will help to manage your stress around the times that you have to hand work in. The students who perform the best are those who are prepared.

If you are not a naturally organised and prepared person, then make sure that you develop a system for recording reminders for yourself. Keep a diary and note down the future deadlines for your assessments and the dates that any drafts of your work need to be submitted. Make regular appointments with your tutor and other members of staff who are available to help you at the university. This will help you to keep on track and nudge you to make sure that you are working on the right thing at the right time.

Keep regular contact with your fellow students – they may have heard something in that lecture which you missed. Set up a social media group so that you can chat about the day's lecture or seminar. This can be really helpful if you need a quick answer to a question in order to get on with your work. Making friends and the social aspect of university are covered more fully in Chapter 3.

This is a whole different world

It takes time to settle into the differences that university presents. Don't worry. Expect to feel unsettled for a while. Give yourself two to three months before you properly begin to feel part of things. It's all new – be patient and keep trying. Keep Calm and Carry on! New students often point out to us that they are surprised that they have to learn so much new vocabulary, both in the subject they are studying and in the wider university. You may be used to teachers and lessons and having to submit coursework but then, all of a sudden, you are attending lectures led by lecturers and have assessment deadlines. You will get used to this change of language; the more you hear and use it, the more comfortable you will feel.

We can't outline here all of the language that you are going to need for the subject you are studying, but you will find an appendix in the back of this book, which is a list of some of the terms used in a wider university context. There is space at the end of the table to add your own words and phrases that you have picked up that are particular to your university or the subject you are studying. There are also questions and prompts after the definitions, so make sure you find the answers to the questions and personalise it, so that it becomes your own quick and easy guide to refer to.

You may be lucky enough to be on a course with a small number of students, but it is common to have lectures alongside 200 other students.

You are embarking on a once-in-a-lifetime experience. Students come to university for a variety of reasons. Some of you will be coming just for the qualification; others may be coming because you want to reach your highest potential in learning. Some of you may want qualifications which lead directly to a job. Whatever the reason, make sure that you make the most of your university experience. In a few years' time, you don't want to be in the position where you look back and have regrets about the time you spent here. Seize every opportunity and take advantage of whatever additional benefits are out there. University is likely to be the most memorable, challenging and enjoyable time of your life – make the most of every moment.

3 SOCIAL LIFE

This chapter is about one of the most important, but (for most people) most worrying aspects of going to university: meeting new people and making new friends.

It's fair to say that having a satisfying social life is high on most students' lists of what they enjoy most about university – and rightly so, because one of the very best things about going to university is becoming life-long friends with people you might never have otherwise met. You might even meet someone special! (The only thing Jodi can remember from her degree induction talk is the Dean of the Faculty saying: 'Right now, without knowing it, some of you are in the same room as your future husband or wife!' Of course, all this did was make everyone in the room surreptitiously check everyone else out. We're still not quite sure what he meant to achieve by this comment, but it did spark a few conversations in the student union bar afterwards!)

This is a silly (but true!) story, but the Dean was on to something. He knew that making friends was most students' top priority. Why might that be? Well, we are social beings (for the most part). Our friendships sustain us, and we take great pleasure in them. When we find life a bit difficult, it is good to have one or two good friends to turn to – to have a laugh with, or a good old moan, to commiserate, or to share ideas. Friendships give us a sense of belonging, and let's be honest, learning is just more fun with others. One of our favourite pastimes is to sit near a group of students studying together in the library or campus café – it is great to see students puzzling over something together, offering their different points of view, sharing their thoughts, helping each other out. It really is the best way to learn.

So, our first piece of advice is to be open to making friends with people who you might never have encountered in the 'outside world'. In one of the modules we have recently taught, there is one particular friendship group that demonstrates how wonderful university can be for widening your social circle. The friendship group is made up of a Hindu female in her late 40s with three teenaged children, a white ex-dental nurse, a white male in his early 20s, an Afro-Caribbean single mother in her late 20s, and an ex-legal assistant (white female, early 30s). We detail the backgrounds of these students only to make this point: these students may have a wide range of backgrounds and experiences, but through university they have found so much common ground. They have banded together to support each other, giving advice and motivating each other (by all accounts they have a lively WhatsApp group).

Take a look around your classes. Who looks interesting? Who haven't you spoken to already? Who looks very different to yourself? This is the time to break out of your friend comfort zone.

Meeting new people is often the best aspect of studying at university

How to make friends if you are shy (this may involve cake)

It is common to struggle to establish friendships, especially if you have joined a course late or miss some lectures and seminars, or because you haven't yet gelled with anybody. One of the main issues with university study is that it is very easy to feel lost in a crowd. There are so many other students (most universities have tens of thousands of students) that it is easy to feel isolated, or that you don't belong, especially if you haven't yet made many friends. Isolation is sometimes a problem if your background is different from the majority of students on the course. It can be really upsetting when this happens. However, don't take it personally – they don't know you, so it can't be personal. Try not to appear defensive – smile and make eye contact - and try to engage someone who looks friendly in small talk. Have a couple of conversation-starters up your sleeve.

Here are a few to get you started:

- Compliment your neighbour on their bag/top/shoes.
- Ask them a straightforward question ('I'm here for module X, are you here for this module, too?')
- Discuss your course ('I'm finding this module really interesting/intriguing/challenging – how about you?')

Asking these sorts of questions can help to break the ice when everyone is feeling self-conscious and a little awkward. Enthusiastically taking part in group tasks in seminars is also helpful, as this is a natural opportunity to speak to new people – you may well be asked to work with students you haven't had the chance to speak to yet, and you have a ready-made icebreaker in the form of the task you have been given to do. So, this is a very good way of connecting with someone new.

Another way to forge friendships is to join university societies. There are societies for all sorts of interests, so joining a society relating to your interests will definitely help you meet like-minded people, from all university years, so this can really widen your social circle. If there isn't a society that reflects one of your interests, start your own! One of our colleagues, who was a student at our university, started a ukulele society in his first year with a friend. He never actually managed to learn how to play a ukulele, but he did make lots of friends through the society! The ukulele society still exists too, even though he graduated a few years ago, as newer students have kept it going.

Universities put on lots of extra-curricular activities – it can be hard to engage with this if you have lots of responsibilities, but still, look for stuff that you can attend. This is a great way to network and make new friends. Just smiling at someone is often enough to get a conversation started – remember, everyone is in the same boat and most people will be receptive to a conversation starter. Some lecturers will include 'icebreaker' activities in their first session with the group; throw yourself into them and at the very least, you can bond with each other over how lame these activities are!

Housemates

One of the biggest challenges of university is having to live alongside people you have never met before (obviously we're talking to those of you who will be living in halls).

Here are some tips for getting on with your housemates. You will notice that these tips focus on you and how you behave. This is because we can only really control our own behaviour and because fallings-out and arguments never help improve the situation.

- Be mindful of those around you: tidy up after yourself when using communal areas.
- Keep noise to a minimum, especially late at night.
- In the first few days: make a nameplate for your door and leave your door open (when you are there, of course) so it is inviting for people to pop in to say hello.

Look for common ground and when you speak to people, be open and friendly. A good way of achieving this is by being interested in your new housemates. Ask them about their pre-university life, what they are studying, where they are from…

Cake is a fantastic way to break the ice, especially if you are living in halls. Throw together a brownie mix, stick it in the oven, and open the kitchen door so the delicious baking smells tempt hungry passers-by to pop in and say hello. Jodi tried this on her first evening in halls (a teacher from sixth-form had recommended the technique to her) and it worked amazingly well – once her flatmates had been lured to the kitchen by the delicious smell of the brownies cooking, they started to get to know each other. After a couple of hours of talking (and eating!) they had the confidence to knock on the door of the flat opposite to introduce themselves (it's always easier to do these things in a group). So, get baking!

A few words of caution

Another thing you should know is that in the first few weeks you will make at least one friend that you will spend the rest of your degree *avoiding*. So, our first piece of advice is not to get locked into friendship groups too early on – keep seeking out new connections. The chances are that you will encounter new people in each module, so every time you start a new module, make the effort to speak to someone new. Be careful about giving too much personal information straight away. Sometimes, being in a new and unknown environment can mean that we become close to people really quickly. Although this can be a beautiful thing, it is sensible to keep a bit of a distance. It can take a while for people's true personalities to emerge, so don't divulge all of your secrets too quickly. Try to figure out the person first – can they be trusted? Also, becoming too friendly with people too quickly can lead to a limited social group. Keep open to the idea of meeting new people throughout your degree, so you can benefit from having a wide range of friends. Keeping yourself out there has additional benefits: the next new person you meet might be the next Mark Zuckerberg. Networking is a more practical reason for making the effort to meet lots of new people. You don't know where your classmates' careers will end up. It's likely that some will be very successful in their future careers, and friendships that are forged at university can lead to great things.

Tip: Surround yourself with similarly-motivated students - create a study-buddy group. You can share ideas, meet for study sessions, and support each other through the ups and downs of life as an undergraduate.

Your lecturers

This section is about that most curious of creatures, the academic. It will attempt to illuminate some of the characters you might encounter at university and will give you an insight into how to get the most out of them.

Lecturers are a mixed bunch, as is any group of humans. Some will very much enjoy teaching. The media peddle the myth that lecturers view teaching as an irritating interruption to their real work - their research. However, you will find that most lecturers appreciate working with lively, engaged students. In our experience, the vast majority of lecturers respond enthusiastically when students demonstrate they are interested, enthusiastic and committed. (This doesn't mean that they respond only to the 'perfect' student, but in reality lecturers want all students who try their best to succeed).

Lecturers come in a variety of shapes and sizes, as this handy table will demonstrate:

	Who they are	How they can help you
Personal Tutor	Most lecturers are also personal tutors. You will be allocated a personal tutor. They should contact you to introduce themselves and to ask you to come and meet them for an informal chat – make sure you go to meet them.	Advice, guidance and support on personal and academic matters. Will write job references for you when you leave university, so it is a good idea to build a positive relationship with them.
Module Leader	They are the lecturer in charge of the module. They are senior members of staff.	They will answer your questions about the module.
PhD student/Graduate Teaching Assistant	Most PhD students want to be lecturers and so will get some teaching experience.	They can be very supportive and happy to help. Likely to have been an undergraduate student themselves recently so they know what it is like!
Course Leader	The lecturer in charge of the whole course. You will probably be taught by them at several points during their course.	They will answer your questions about the course.
Senior Lecturer/ Reader Professor/Principal Lecturer	Senior members of staff with a good academic standing. You might be taught by them.	They will pass on their hard-earned expertise.
The Dean	The equivalent of the 'headmaster' of the Faculty.	You might be taught by them, but then again, you might never see them!

At some point in your studies, you will find yourself in a lecturer's office. At the very least, you will be allocated a member of the lecturing staff as your personal tutor, so you will be expected to go to see them in their office for a chat. Some lecturers will hold seminars in their office, or you might need to pop in because you have a question or want feedback on an assignment. Ideally, you will want to speak to your lecturer because you love your subject and have a strong need to talk about it with someone who really knows their stuff.

Whatever the reason for your being in their office, it pays to observe your surroundings. There will be piles, and piles, and piles of books – on shelves, on the floor, on the only free seat in the room. There will be old posters on the wall with curling edges, some of them displaying the lecturer's name – evidence of some learned event they have organised. Their door will display their office hours on an A4 sheet (for the last academic year - don't expect them to make it easy for you to track them down). There might be tea-and-coffee-making facilities, comprising a kettle, a bottle of 16p own-brand value bottled water, and a heavily tea-stained cup.

Not all offices are like this, of course. Some are modern, and ultra-organised – clean and tidy. These are the lecturers to watch out for. They are ruthless, ambitious, and probably hard markers 😁.

Lecturers are people too!

It can be quite intimidating to be on the lecturer's turf: up-close-and-personal. But, remember – your lecturer is human, too! They are probably as stressed/more stressed than you – perhaps just for different reasons.

Don't be surprised if you actually enjoy talking to your lecturers – we enjoy talking to you. You will find that we treat you as an adult, and that immature behaviour is met with confusion. We find that we have far-ranging conversations with our students, as you might with a friend. Be mindful that it isn't a real friendship, though, and it is sensible and right for both you and the lecturer to keep a professional distance. It is not a good idea for students and staff to get over-involved with each other – lecturers are best viewed as an academic resource rather than a source of emotional support.

Lecturers come in all shapes and sizes!

Office hours

Your lecturers will have office hours. These are specific times in the week where they must be available to speak to students. In our experience, only a small number of students use office hours, and these students gain an advantage. They ask questions about the course content, or get feedback on their writing. Use office hours judiciously to advance your learning through discussion with your lecturers.

How to get lecturers to do what you want via email

Yes, email is still the main communication method of choice at university (we know, so 1990s). You will need to email your lecturers at some point – usually to ask them for some information or to answer a question you have, etc. Lecturers get loads of emails and usually have a target 'turnaround' for emails: in other words, they must respond to emails within a set period of time (think days, though, rather than hours). So, emails tend to be the bane of their lives, especially emails that are badly written or vague.

So, here are the essential rules to stop lecturers hating emails:

- Remember, emails are not instant messages/Snapchat/WhatsApp. One-line emails with no introduction (so no 'dear so-and-do') are a sure-fire way of getting their backs up. Over-deliver on the 'pleases' and 'thank yous'.

- Write in formal English. Be concise – but not blunt.

- Don't expect instant answers to emails. If it's really urgent, try to find them on campus for a quick word.

- But send polite reminders if/when you don't get a response within a reasonable time (think days/a week, not hours).

- Don't email in the middle of the night – and if you do, don't expect a response first thing in the morning, or on a Sunday morning.

- Don't email when angry.

- Don't email when drunk.

- Give them the info they need to help you – student ID number, name of module, day/time module meets.

- Don't email asking questions which you could find out the answers to yourself, by reading stuff like module guides/syllabus.

Don't take it personally if you get a one-line response to your carefully-crafted email, weeks after you sent it, complete with 'Sent from my iPhone' sign-off. (They are busy people, you know.)

So, a bad example of an email would be:

Why am I not on the register?

There are obvious problems with this email – putting aside the fact that its bluntness could easily be interpreted as rudeness, there are other issues – there is not enough information for the lecturer to be able to help, for a start. Remember, you are likely to be one of hundreds of students that the lecturer teaches. They will need a lot more to go on than that. Think writing a letter, rather than sending a message on WhatsApp.

A good example would be:

Dear Dr. Bloggs

I am a student in XXX module, which you teach on Tuesday mornings. My student number is xxxxxxx. I have noticed that I am not on the register and Student Support told me that I should contact you to get my name added. I would really appreciate it if you could look into this for me.

Best wishes, A. Student

Why is the second email better? It includes the details the lecturer will need to help you: your student ID, the module and class you are in and there is evidence that you have tried to solve the problem yourself. Plus, it is polite and written carefully.

Student Support

In most universities these days, the academics are outnumbered by administrative staff. These guys are unsung heroes. They know more about the university than the lecturers do. They can help with finance, accommodation, timetables, registering your programme, university regulations, extensions, and assessment submissions – in other words, everything apart from the actual learning.

Now, depending on your luck, if you do need help from student support you will experience one of two types of student advisers. The first type can be characterised as dismissive, abrupt, visibly irritated by your very presence, and unhelpful: in other words, the type of person who should never be let loose in a 'customer service' role. The other type of student adviser can be a life-saver; knowledgeable, helpful, and sympathetic. Try to work out who is who – knowing who is helpful and having a named person to go to for help is very useful.

Find out where to go for help for practical matters as soon as you get to university – don't wait until you are stressed and need their help, as trying to work out who can help will only add to your stress levels, at a time when you really don't need the extra stress.

Making group-work work

At some point in your degree, it is pretty inevitable that you will be asked to work collaboratively with some of your fellow students. This might be something as simple as discussing a point in class, to devising and giving a group presentation, or carrying out an in-depth project. It's been known for medical students to practise taking blood from each other, but that might be a little extreme.

It's fair to say that most students dislike group work, especially if your individual grades are based on the group effort. A popular meme characterises typical group members along these lines: '…Every group project: The one who does 99% of the work. The one who has no idea what is going on. The one who says they are going to help but never does. And the one who disappears at the very beginning and doesn't show up again until the very end'.

Managing group work is tricky, even more so if you don't get to choose group members. However, this doesn't mean you can't make a success of it. There are even some benefits to it. Here are some ideas on how you can make the most of your peers:

- Make clear decisions about who needs to do what, and by when.
- Use social media to make plans if you can't meet in person regularly.
- Don't be a martyr and do the extra work if your colleagues don't produce the goods. Make it clear to the lecturer what your contribution was.
- Decide to do well and make your high expectations known to the rest of the group.

Enjoy working with your peers and make the most of the opportunity. Group work can be challenging, but it can also be fun, and you can learn more from working with other people than you would on your own.

This is our final tip to round off this chapter: if you only do one thing, be brave and make yourself known to your lecturers early on. This will help you in so many useful ways.

4 LOOKING AFTER YOURSELF

For some students, going to university will just be a busier than usual time of life with no major impact on the level of their responsibilities (for example mature students), but for other students who are perhaps moving away from home for the first time to live in shared accommodation or halls of residence, the priorities and pressures of independent living can take their toll. It is our aim in this chapter to talk you through some of the additional responsibilities that you may have as a student and also to provide some useful hints, tips and shortcuts to caring for yourself and being at the peak of your 'wellness' for the journey ahead.

Mindfulness

We're not entirely sure if we like the term 'mindfulness' or not – sometimes it makes us think of a load of hippies meditating in the sunshine in a field, at other times we just imagine that it is a general state of mind. We're not sure that anyone really knows what mindfulness actually is, so instead we're going to offer up a bit of advice on keeping your head on track or keeping focused on what really matters – you! You are what really matters to you. In order to keep a healthy mind, you may wish to turn your attention to a couple of very short and easy-to-do exercises:

Exercise 1: Pay attention to an everyday object for one minute. It doesn't matter what the object is. Look at the object in the present moment. Don't think about the object, don't analyse the object. Just stay in the present moment.

Exercise 2: Close your eyes and concentrate on breathing for one minute. Be conscious of the moment. Take slow, deep breaths – three seconds in, then three seconds out.

We are not saying that we know any more than a couple of interesting tips on keeping our heads. But it has come to our attention that a simple awareness of awareness is helpful. Try it. Sometimes the 'present moment' gets squeezed out of our life. Sometimes we are so busy analysing what happened in the past and planning what will happen in the future that we spend little or no time on the present. And the present is all that we really have. It is important that, in order to study effectively, our mind is aware of its relationship with the outside world. This will help us to navigate our way through and open up our minds to be able to learn effectively and efficiently.

In addition to the mind exercises described above, you may want to Google some very simple stretching exercises. Being a student can be a very sedentary life; you're always sitting at a computer, reading and writing. Take time out to realise that you have one body and one mind and that they need attention too.

Staying Clean

We can't study and work hard if we don't look after ourselves and the environment around us. We will speak a little in Chapter 6 about prioritising cleaning duties in the home. As well as keeping a clean space to be able to work in, we need a clean body and a clean mind. Don't let your personal hygiene slip: take regular baths or showers and always make sure that you are 'presentable'. We don't mean that you have to get dressed up in your best clothes every day to attend your lectures, not at all. But when you walk out of your accommodation in the morning ready to start the day, make sure that you are presented so that, for example, you wouldn't mind meeting your Head of Department on the street. You wouldn't want to be too embarrassed to say hello because you were wearing that old t-shirt that Auntie Jenny bought you five years ago that has clearly seen better days. Wash your clothes regularly and change your pants and socks every day! This may sound silly or obvious, but it's important and it's smelly and unhygienic if you don't (no more mum rant for the time being).

Exercise

There is a free body and mind 'boost' which is available to all of us. It's the endorphin release we feel when we move around. Chemicals are released in our body when we do any form of exercise and these chemicals have been proven to increase our wellness and wellbeing. They are the 'happy' chemicals which allow us to feel good. Get some of these chemicals racing round your body at least once a day. It's not our job here to tell you to join the gym or rugby team, neither are we qualified to be telling you exactly what type of exercise you should be doing – that's up to you. Most of us have a step counter on our mobile phones; 10,000 steps every day is a good guide to how much walking you should be doing. Have a look at your phone now, how many steps did you do yesterday? Are you happy with that amount? We've just looked at our phones and found that we only did 6,500 each yesterday. What a disgrace! We've made an agreement that we'll walk a bit further today. Sally has decided to walk home today, and Jodi's promised that she'll walk the dog before going out for a meal tonight. Endorphins galore!

Answer the questions below, to start thinking about how to build exercise into your new university routine:

- What exercise do you think will suit your university routine?
- How can you increase your daily steps?
- Are there clubs or societies at your university that you fancy joining? What are they and how can you join?
- How much is gym membership at your university? University gym membership prices may surprise you. Is this something that you would be interested in?

Jot down three ways in which you will be able to make your daily routine a bit more active. For example, 'I'm going to walk to university in future instead of getting the bus'; 'I'm going to make sure that I climb the two sets of stairs to my lecture theatre instead of waiting for the lift'. Changes that you decide on now may positively impact the way that you live and learn throughout your time at university.

Ways in which I am going to change my routine to be more active:

1.

2.

3.

'Should I take the lift...or the stairs? Perhaps I'll toss a coin'

Drinking and drugs

Whilst in the past university used to mean endless nights of seeing how you could out-drink your fellow class mates in order to 'bond' over the experience, times have changed. You must take very great care in the consumption of alcohol. It's not healthy and it can be very dangerous. Alcohol costs more than money. Every year we hear a story of a student who has gone to university and through no fault of his/her own has had a life-threatening experience because of drinking too much. Please don't let this be you. Drink in moderation and always make sure that you are in a safe environment whilst you are drinking. Make sure that you watch the company that you keep, don't drink with people you wouldn't normally spend time with. Always have the means to get home; don't even dream of spending your last £10 on beer if you then can't afford your taxi fare.

So that's a word on safety but here follows a cautionary financial warning. Alcohol, because of the huge taxes in Britain, is extremely expensive. Think what else you could buy for the price of that pint of beer! In fact, we want you to do more than just think about it; write down below how much three pints of beer would cost and in the opposite column think of the things that you would be able to buy with the same amount of money.

Examples could include lunch for you and a mate, two days' groceries or a train ticket to somewhere you need or want to go.

Price of three pints of beer (or your favourite tipple):	I would rather spend this money on:

We hope that by filling in the table above you have seen what an utter waste of money drinking alcohol is. There are far better things to spend your very precious money on.

Now we are afraid that we are going to turn our attention to drugs. Drugs (unless prescribed by a doctor) are dangerous and cost far, far more than money. We have (as lecturers) been aware of students who have thrown away their chances of a university education because of drugs. If you are found in possession of drugs on university premises then, depending on the disciplinary procedures of your university, you will either be reprimanded or excluded. We have also seen (too many times) students who are unable to attend lectures or to engage in normal university life because taking or smoking drugs has become the focus of their time.

Don't do it. Don't succumb to any pressure from those around you. Resist the taking of drugs: always. If you think that you may have a problem with drugs or alcohol, please seek out the help that you need and then get the support that will enable you to live the life that you want at university.

Eating

We're sure you don't need us to bang on in this book about getting your five a day, you're probably bored of this old message. But you're not going to be able to avoid a bit of a foodie lecture! Eating well is the foundation to good health, an active body and a sharp brain. These three things underpin your success at university. Yes, really! There is no way you can study well and learn and succeed at university without taking care of your body and mind, so we're going to give you a few dos and don'ts regarding your eating. Stick to these rules and you will build the right foundations for success at university.

It is remarkable that the people in Pioppi, Italy live, on average, 10 years longer than people here in the UK. They are much healthier than us; they have a lower incidence of heart disease and diabetes which are the two great killers in the UK. A lot of research has been carried out as to why this is the case. It found that the Pioppi diet is full of nuts, seeds, fruit and veg and contains absolutely no processed foods, and therefore we can perhaps conclude that this is one of the healthiest diets to follow.

So, this has to be the foundation of what we eat. Ditch the processed foods. A processed food is any food which has had 'something done to it'. These can vary immensely; there is kind of a level of badness which can be attached to each processed food. At the 'not very harmful' level are things like ready-washed spinach and frozen vegetables. At the 'very harmful' level, which is what we must aim to avoid, are things like ready meals, shop-bought pizza, and meats with high levels of salt, such as sausages and bacon. Try to avoid these foods, if possible. They are harmful to your body and the consumption of these foods will not allow you to achieve your potential at university.

Ditch the take-aways and ready meals. Believe it or not, the producers of 'fast' foods create their recipes with the aim of getting you hooked on their produce. They set out to provide you with a 'bliss' point in a product. The bliss point is the point at which you feel the ultimate pleasure, with not too much and not too little salt, sugar or fat. These foods, once tasted, are really difficult to resist.

Kick the habit: Me: 1, Manufacturers: 0. You are the winner in every way: financially and nutritionally.

Here are our top tips to winning in the fight against being a slave to junk food and convenience rubbish eating:

- Plan what you are going to eat for the week ahead at a time which is appropriate to you (maybe at the weekend when you have some free time). Perhaps do a bit of batch cooking and freeze the delicious things that you have cooked (see page 41 for more info on batch cooking).

- Go shopping – find the cheapest supermarket near you and off you go. Fill your basket with fresh produce, fruit, vegetables, nuts and lean meats and fish. Buy some eggs. Look on the bottom shelves of the supermarkets for the real bargains. Make sure you are eating good sources of protein – canned fish (cheapish), chicken, lean meat, eggs, nuts, pulses, beans.

- Make sure you eat lots of different coloured foods. A meal containing purple beetroot, orange carrot, brown rice and white chicken breast is sure to give you a boost

- Leave the take-away and fast food manufacturers to fend for themselves – you don't need this food. You will get more out of your time at university if you ditch the manufacturers' tricks. Cook!

Where and how to shop

Many students, before going to university, have never had to spend their own money on the weekly grocery shopping. There is an important lesson of 'how to shop for food' which some of us never learn. Below we will outline a couple of tricks in order to get you started. You'll soon get the hang of it and perhaps even enjoy it!

Sally took her young daughter to the supermarket in the summer holidays. She gave her £5 to spend on anything that she wished but said to her daughter that she must be able (with Mum's help) create two meals for herself out of the ingredients. This didn't go well; her maths skills weren't up to scratch and her idea of nutrition left something to be desired. She filled her shopping basket with doughnuts and sweets and an apple. She spent £2.56. When they arrived home and Sally asked her what ideas she had to create her meals, her daughter's face dropped. Sally agreed to prepare her meals for her that day and that they would try the same project tomorrow. Sally spoke to her about what ingredients she might need to feel full and have a healthy body. Tomorrow came and this time Sally's daughter meant business. She went straight to the reduced fruit and vegetables and picked up a bargain pack of carrots, some reduced-price rice noodles and some broccoli, then marched off to the ready-cooked chickens and bought a half chicken. Next, she selected yogurts, pasta, bread and a tin of spaghetti hoops. All for under a fiver.

The point in us telling you this story is not to embarrass Sally's daughter, but to show you that we need to teach ourselves how to shop. It is not a talent that we are born with.

Supermarkets (we know this is true of Sainsbury's, Asda, Tesco, Morrison's and M&S) tend to reduce the price of some of their items a couple of hours before the store closes. Find out what time your local supermarket closes and locate where they usually place their reduced-priced items. Some supermarkets reduce all of their fresh produce to as little as 10p once they have reached their sell-by date. But you have to be in the know. You have to learn where and when this is going to happen, and you have to be quick - there are other savvy customers out there who want YOUR bargain!

Make the bulk of your purchases at a budget supermarket (Aldi, Lidl or Jack's). These places really are about 20% cheaper than the big supermarkets. And the quality these days is about the same as the other big supermarkets. The choice may be more limited, but this doesn't matter. Make sure that in your first shopping trip you buy the basic store cupboard ingredients that you will need to get you started. This shopping trip will be a bit more expensive than future weeks, but don't worry, you will use these ingredients over and over again.

Store cupboard ingredients: add to the list below *before you go to the supermarket* if there is something that you think you will need (we've left a couple of spaces at the end for you to fill in). Stick to your list when shopping; don't fall for any of the supermarket three for two offers.

- A selection of herbs, spices and stock cubes to your taste and salt and pepper, tomato puree.

- Flour, for baking cakes (perhaps those delicious brownies we talked about in Chapter 3). Dried pasta and rice (remember to look on the bottom shelves of the supermarket for the best value).

- Eggs, cheese, UHT milk, butter or margarine, wholemeal bread, flour tortillas.

- Tins: tuna fish, sweetcorn, baked beans, tomatoes, chickpeas, other cheap pulses in tins, supermarket own brand tinned fruit.

- Fresh vegetables, fruit and salad (Is there a market near you? What days of the week does the market operate? Fresh fruit and vegetables are normally cheaper when bought from the market).

- From the freezer: chicken portions, minced beef, fish portions, any frozen veg that you fancy. Frozen mashed potato is delicious - try it.

-

-

Below are a few recipe ideas of meals you should be able to cook quickly and easily without breaking the bank.

Lime Chicken and Rice

Put two or three frozen chicken portions in a deep baking tray on a bed of uncooked rice. Add twice as much water as rice. Add salt, pepper, a crumbled stock cube, lemon zest and chilli, if you like it. Cover with silver foil and bake in a medium hot oven for one hour. Check that the rice hasn't dried out after half an hour and add more water if needed. Lift the foil for the last 10 minutes of cooking in order to brown the chicken.

Chicken Fajitas

Cut chicken breast pieces into strips and fry with peppers and onions, chopped garlic, chilli powder and paprika, salt and pepper to taste. If you like a saucy fajita, then add a little flour to the chicken mix when frying and a tin of chopped tomatoes. Cook all this together for about 10 minutes. Wrap in flour tortillas and serve. This recipe can be used for Mexican burritos too. Simply take the wrapped tortillas stuffed with your chicken, pepper and onion mix, place in an oven proof bowl, sprinkle with grated cheese and bake in a medium oven for 10 minutes.

Cheese Toastie Cheat

Toasted sandwiches are delicious. People often think that you cannot make a toastie without a griddle machine. Well, you can. Simply make your cheese sandwich but be sure to put the butter or spread on the outside of the bread, not the inside. Place this sandwich in a frying pan (no need for any oil as you have your butter on your bread) on a low heat for a couple of minutes. Turn the sandwich over and allow to cook for a further two minutes. Try this with different ingredients: beans, ham, onions, and tuna all work well - use your imagination!

Basic Tuna Pasta Bake

Cook pasta (any pasta shape will do, although avoid spaghetti as it tends to dry out in the oven) until it is al dente; this simply means it still has a bit of bite to the texture. Drain the pasta and add a tin of tuna, some tinned sweetcorn, half a tin of tomatoes, salt and pepper, garlic and chilli sauce, if you wish. Place in an ovenproof bowl and sprinkle with cheese. Cook for 15 minutes in the middle of a medium hot oven for 15 minutes or until it is golden brown on top. This recipe can be adapted to use tinned chickpeas instead of pasta or can be eaten on its own on top of a baked potato.

Saving time and money by batch cooking

Dishes like the pasta bake, burritos, and lime chicken and rice can all be cooked in larger quantities, allowed to cool and then frozen in individual containers. This is called batch cooking. You can then just take a meal out of the freezer a couple of hours before you want to eat it - heat it up in a microwave when it's fully defrosted. Remembering to cook an extra two or three extra portions for the freezer every week will definitely save you time and money.

In this chapter we have looked at aspects of taking care of ourselves - our body and our mind - in order that we achieve to our full potential at university. There is a lot more help on these aspects on the internet.

Try searching for such things as:

What to eat at university
How to eat well for just £10 a week
Five steps to eating well at university
James Smith Food and Diet
Preparing to Go – the Complete University Guide
Do university students need more exercise?

The answer doesn't lie in this book or these websites. The answer lies with you. Decide how you want to 'be' at university, live happy and well and adapt the material that you have read through in this book and the websites to suit your own life. Making small changes now to your mindfulness, exercise, diet and consumption of alcohol will make your whole student experience a brighter and more balanced one. As a consequence of this, you will have a happier and more successful experience.

5 MONEY

In this chapter, we will suggest some ideas to help you manage your money – a topic that is of great interest to students, as there never seems to be enough to go around!

First of all, a disclaimer: the following information does not constitute financial advice. It is some useful hints and tips gathered over a few years of experience.

For most students, going into further study is a massive financial commitment. At the very least, there are the thousands of pounds of tuition fees and maintenance loans that will need to be borrowed.

If you are going back into education after a period of time working and have become used to earning money, having a smaller income may be a shock to the system.

Some of you will have to start budgeting your money for the first time. If you are in this category, prepare to be shocked by the prices of the following essential items:

- Toilet paper

- Laundrettes and/or washing powder[3]

- Single items of anything from a local shop

We imagine that all of you have carefully worked out the sums to find out how much money you will need for university. Even if the figures suggest that, on paper, you will have enough cash to get by; don't underestimate the power of money (or, rather, a lack of it). It is essential that you pay(!) close attention to your cash flow from the beginning of your studies. Money has a way of causing problems in the future if it is not managed well in the present.

Student finance

Apply for student finance as early as possible. Your parents may need to share their income details as part of your application. If you are a mature student, applications for finance can be more complicated, due to complex family finances, so the earlier you apply, the better. Delays on the first payment due in September are unfortunately very common, and depending on the reason for the delay, it can take time to sort out and get your first payment through. Assume the first payment will be late and plan accordingly. Make sure you (or your parents) have original copies of key paperwork (P60s, passports, etc.) in place before you apply, so that you can get the information to student finance as promptly as possible. Keep all your reference numbers/passwords safe as you will need to log back in to reapply for finance for each new year of study.

---

[3] Tip: take your own washing powder with you to the launderette, don't pay their extortionate prices!

Working out your budget

Once you know whether you will be in receipt of a maintenance loan and how much that loan will be, you should draw up a budget. Student loan payments are issued three times a year (around September, January and April) which isn't really helpful in terms of budgeting, especially if you are used to being paid on a weekly or monthly basis. You will need to make sure you have enough cash to pay for your monthly bills, even in month 4, way after your last payment. The most annoying thing about the timing of the student loan payments is that the last one of the academic year is in April, and the next payment won't be until the end of September – that makes five months between payments. Have you a plan for these months?

Like the time management exercise suggested in Chapter 6, it is a sensible idea to work out what added pressures there will be on your finances, for example Christmas, summer holidays, and friends' and family's birthdays.

Budget planning

Use this budget planner to get a realistic idea of how much money you have to spend on a weekly/monthly basis and how you may have to spend your money.

Use the planner below to estimate what your costs will be for the typical bills students have to pay:

1. What is your total income per term (Student Finance usually splits the payment into three - do you know when to expect the money?)

2. Now you know when you will receive the loan, how long do you need to make it last until the next payment (divide loan amount by number of months until the next payment):

3. Now work out your income per week:

4. Next, take a look at the bills below. You might need to pay for some of these monthly, or even upfront on a termly basis. Have a think about how you will manage these costs.

Use the table below to start your planning.

Typical bills	Cost per month or week
Accommodation and bills	
Travel/commuting	
TV Licence	
Mobile phone	
Personal care and grooming	
Groceries (including cleaning supplies, washing powder)	
Socialising	
Entertainment (Netflix, etc.)	
Clothes	
Launderette[4]	
TOTAL	

How well does your budget balance? Are there any areas in which you will need to be especially careful?

Student money-saving ideas

1. Minimise eating on campus

We consider food on campus to be pretty expensive – the days of the cheap student union are well behind us. Instead, franchises such as Starbucks and Costa often have a presence on campus, and they aren't any cheaper than the high street. Do you really need to have a Starbucks every time you go to university – could you take your own coffee in a flask? Is £4 for a lunch meal deal really a good deal? Small costs add up dramatically. A meal deal and a coffee would cost around £7 a day – that's £35 a week! Just on lunch! You could feed yourself for a week with that – see Chapter 4 for some cheap but tasty and nutritious recipes. At the time of writing this book, Tesco were advertising the ingredients for spaghetti bolognaise or fish, chips and peas and salad for four people for under £5.

---

[4] No, you can't take all your dirty washing home for Mum or Dad to do it!

Bringing a packed lunch from home can save you a lot of money

2. Books

Don't buy new books: go through your reading list early and get key books from the library. Keep an eye out for students selling their used textbooks. Older editions of books are usually cheaper, and the content doesn't usually change dramatically between editions.

3. Technology

A basic laptop is good enough if your subject only really requires you to access the internet and type up work. Most universities give you a free downloadable copy of Microsoft Office.

4. Free food

If you volunteer for various things (helping out at open days, etc.) you can get free food and sometimes payment.

5. Student discounts

The National Union of Student's TOTUM card costs a few quid, but it can pay for itself in one use. You can get a TOTUM card from your student union. It's really good for saving money at the cinema, eating out and fashion. Your student ID card can also get you discounts in loads of places – sometimes just being cheeky and asking if there are any discounts for students can pay off. Keep your student ID on you at all times. We always carry ours and we aren't afraid to ask if retailers offer student discounts.

6. Save money when food shopping

Focus on minimising grocery bills – see Chapter 4 for some ideas of eating well for less.

Taking on paid work

As selfish lecturers, we don't want you to take on too much paid work as well as your studies. We want you to be able to devote yourselves to your studies. But we do understand that for the majority of students, having paid work is a necessity. The best jobs to work alongside study are either directly related to your subject, or they are roles that are not too demanding, so they don't use up your precious energy. Try to get your employer onside and sympathetic towards some flexibility in hours to suit your university timetable, maybe by letting you take time off at busy times or increasing your hours outside of the semester.

Be careful not to take on too much; do the minimum number of working hours you can manage on. We have had students actually fall asleep during sessions, not because they were bored (we hope!) but because they were utterly exhausted – one student came to a 9a.m. lecture after working through the night. The student was clearly committed (they'd made a massive effort to come to the lecture, after all) but it is not healthy or sustainable to work such extreme hours. Some students work full-time alongside studying full-time. You may need to work a lot of hours to stay afloat, but at the same time beware of the lure of extra money; it can be very beguiling. You may earn extra money, but this will inevitably be at the expense of your studies. If you can accept being relatively skint but make the most of the opportunities university will give you, you are giving yourself the best chance of succeeding and staying healthy.

There are some sources of help if you find yourself in really bad financial shape. All universities will have crisis loans and grants available. There are often extra grants for students in specific categories – parents, care leavers, or students with disabilities. Check out your university's website for information. More positive sources of help include university bursaries and scholarships. These sometimes have strings attached and some of these might exclude some students (e.g. high grades at A Levels) but some might be more inclusive. A final source might be educational grants and scholarships from charitable organisations.

Do a little bit of research and jot down below any useful information you could follow up on to bring in some extra cash:

Is it really worth getting into so much debt to go to university?

The media often reports the staggering amounts of 'debt' students graduate with, and I'm guessing this is a question that you will have asked yourself. Martin Lewis (TV's 'Money Saving Expert') makes an insightful point about student debt: degrees will only cost you what you pay back. So, even though on paper you might graduate 'owing' tens of thousands of pounds, the majority of graduates will only pay back a proportion of their 'debt'. Only the highest earning graduates will pay back the whole amount borrowed. This group has clearly benefited from going to university and can afford to pay it all back. It may help to view the money that you are borrowing as an investment in your future rather than a debt attached to your present. This might help you spend it wisely, too. Regardless of the different opinions on student finance, we think that the debts you should be more worried about are bad debts such as store cards, overdrafts and credit cards, not to mention the dreadful payday loans. The terms for paying these debts back can lead to real hardship. If you do find yourself in financial difficulty, these options may seem like attractive solutions, but they often spiral dangerously out of control, adding extreme amounts of interest. If you feel tempted to borrow from these sources of bad debt, take a step back and look at possible savings you might make. For students, every pound coin matters, and you can only spend it once, so spend it wisely.

So, expect to be skint, but with a little bit of thought, it need not spoil your experience: in fact, you will be developing good habits for the future.

6 TIME

If we had a pound for every student who didn't hand in an assignment on time because they 'hadn't realised it was due in' we would have quite a few pounds! When the semester starts, there will be a lot of different elements to juggle at the same time. You can expect multiple end-of-semester assignment deadlines and revision for exams, as well as weekly tasks such as preparing for seminars, lab work/practicals, going to lectures, etc.

When life gets busy, it is easier than you think to lose track of what needs to be done and when it needs to be done by. It is likely that being at university will give you more to do, and less time to do it in. Or, on the flip side, it might seem that you have too much free time, as life at university is much less structured than college life or work. This can be a dangerous illusion.

Spend time, don't waste it – three years will fly by!

It doesn't matter how bright/intelligent/quick to learn you are: if you are disorganised it will affect your achievement. Universities will routinely penalise late assessments, most often by automatically allocating a grade of 0%. This should be motivation enough to make sure you don't miss deadlines.

So, what can you do to stay on top of things? How about using an Information Hub?

Your Information Hub

An Information Hub is somewhere (outside of your head) where you keep a record of all the stuff you need to do. It is crucial that you only have one Information Hub – home, work, and study all in one place. Having more than one increases the chance of something being missed. Having just one is therefore more efficient. The perfect Information Hub is the good old diary/planner. It can be electronic or on paper, whatever suits you. And before you say anything, diaries aren't just for teenage girls; they are for everybody who wants to succeed. Think about it: every CEO of a large corporation employs someone to manage their diary – if their commitments aren't managed effectively, they are not going to be successful. Are you lucky enough to have a personal assistant? If not, perhaps now is a good time to take control and focus on being more organised.

Personally, we prefer a paper diary as we find it easier to scribble in appointments. We also find we are more likely to jot down other bits of useful information too – ideas, names of books, etc. Use whatever works for you. If you always have your mobile with you, it makes sense to use that as your Information Hub. Keep it on you at all times and update it whenever something comes up. Set yourself some (achievable) short and long-term targets and tick them off as you complete them. The key thing is to get into the habit of updating and reviewing your schedule on a daily and weekly basis, starting from the very beginning of the semester (or whenever it is that you are reading this – it's never too late to start).

This should keep you on track; it is incredibly motivating to see just how far you have progressed. When you inevitably feel that it is all too much, you have a ready-made plan of action which will help you feel more in control.

The following exercise will guide you through organising your time on a semester basis (it is a good idea to take a semester-long view as you will have a different timetable each semester, so trying to plan for the whole year isn't worth it).

You will need your diary (sorry, Information Hub) to hand.

Your time management action plan

Semester-long planning

At the start of each new semester, note the following:

- Semester start and finish dates.
- Dates of any breaks in your lecture timetable.
- All assessment deadlines, including exam dates, if known. If not, note the exam weeks – plan to be available.
- Note resit deadlines/resit exam weeks - it's a good idea to know when they are.
- Writing down this information makes it real and anchors it in your memory – you are much more likely to remember them, even without the prompts in your diary.

Next, make a note of any significant dates that are coming up in your personal life:

- Religious festivals, holy days and observances.

- Significant special events: weddings, anniversaries, Uncle John's 60th birthday, etc.

- Holidays (including children's school holidays and inset days, if applicable).

Sit back and survey where these dates have fallen. Are there any clashes where you will have a lot going on at the same time? You can expect the majority of your module assessments to be due at the same time, so you need to be prepared for this. Make a careful note of any mid-module assessments, too. How will you manage these conflicts?

Weekly planning

Now, the following exercise will build on the last task and help you visualise how your week will jigsaw together. Once you can visualise this, you will be able to make some conscious decisions about how you use your time on a weekly basis. Together with the dates you have already identified, you will be able to loosely plan how you will fit everything in.

You are going to plan out a weekly schedule (including weekends) with your fixed (predictable and routine) personal commitments. A simple grid works best:

	9am	10am	11am	12pm	1pm	2pm	3pm	4pm	5pm
Mon	Lectures			Library				Gym	
Tues					Lectures				
Wed	Work								
Thurs	Lectures				Food shopping				
Fr		Lectures							
Sat					Work				
Sun	Relax								Laundry

Your fixed commitments are likely to include:

- Any caring responsibilities
- Housework and laundry
- Shopping, cooking and meal times
- Paid work/volunteering
- Socialising
- Relaxation and exercise
- Sleep
- Hobbies

Next, add the following to your grid:

- Lectures and seminars
- Commuting time

You may have noticed that there is one category not yet allocated: your independent study time. You need to find around 20 hours a week, as a full-time student, for your independent study.

How is your week looking? How much blank space is there (i.e. time you haven't allocated yet)? Are you surprised (and perhaps a little dismayed) by how little time you have 'free' to allocate to your independent study? But you must make time. Because this is the time when you will do your reading, researching, thinking, and writing; in other words, in terms of your university life, your most crucial activities. You might find that some of your personal fixed commitments will need to move to accommodate your lectures. Try to find another time for them.

It is important to schedule your independent study time for when you are at your best – alert, rested, and when you can study without distraction or interruption. It's no good trying to study when you are tired, hungry, or just haven't got sufficient time.

When do you study best – are you a lark (i.e. you like to get up early) or an owl (i.e. you like to study late at night), for example? When is your house quiet?

Your job now is to work out how you can free up some good quality time. Don't forget, the university year is relatively short, so any sacrifices made will only be for the short-term. Knowing this will make any compromises needed more palatable.

Strategies for freeing up time

These are some ideas of how you can claw back some precious time for your independent study. Remember, you need about 20 hours per week in addition to the 12 you will spend in class.

You will have less time to do the cleaning/chores. That's a fact that will either please or dismay you! If you usually have impeccable standards of cleanliness, now is the time to realise that cleaning and chores are thankless, endless tasks and it doesn't matter if your living space is not at show-house standard. Do enough to get by – you can have a big old clear up at the end of the semester. The only areas that are important keep on top of, on a day-to-day basis, are doing the laundry and keeping bathrooms and kitchens clean. Everything else can be skirted over until you have the time to tackle it properly.

If you are a mature student, this might be the ideal time to review the division of household labour with your partner/kids (if you have them): could they do more? If they can, allocate tasks according to what you each find the least intolerable, then leave them to it.

If you are reading this before you start university, think about having a big clear-out of clutter. Throw out old stuff, give unneeded clothes to charity, get rid of any ornaments that collect dust, or sell items on eBay (minimalism is in!). Less clutter makes it easier to keep your space clean and reduces stress, as it is easier to find the things you actually need, if there is less stuff to start with.

Cooking and shopping can also be streamlined. Create a regular meal schedule – pasta on Mondays, jacket potatoes on Tuesdays, fish on Fridays, a takeaway on Saturdays – you get the idea. This will make day-to-day life a lot simpler, and most of us eat the same old meals, anyway; you're just acknowledging that you have a routine. If you are responsible for cooking for others, we guarantee no-one else will notice if you don't tell them.

For the ultimate in making your life easier, try ordering your shopping online and batch-cooking your family favourites, so that you only need to pull out a frozen home-cooked meal and defrost it in the fridge overnight. Then, at dinnertime, you only need to warm the meal through, add some fresh vegetables, and *bon appetit*. Rinse and repeat for the next day. Tasty, healthy, quick, and cheap. This can free up at least an hour a day. For more on eating well and more tips on looking after yourself whilst at university, pop over to Chapter 4.

Using trapped time

'Trapped time' just means 'gaps between events'. An example of trapped time might be the half-hour between lectures or waiting to go in to see the dentist. Life is full of trapped time. This trapped time can be used to your advantage. When you are on campus, it might be just enough time to check out a book, or print a paper to read, or make some notes for an essay, or review your diary. Keep in mind a list of small jobs that need doing and use this time to get them done.

Get used to making the most of your time

Grouping chores and automating tasks

This means planning when you are going to do your tasks so that you can get several errands done at the same time. This can apply to your home life and to your studies. Go shopping once a week only, and shop at only one shop. If you go into town for the dentist, post those letters and pick up your prescription at the same time. Pick up the books you need from the library on a day when you have to go into university anyway, then there's no need to make a special journey just to pick them up. Listen to a recorded lecture/podcast that has been set as a learning task while you walk the dog/clean the kitchen/go for a run. You get the picture.

Automated tasks can be helpful too. Get all your bills paid by direct debit, on the same day each month, so you only need to check them once. Set up your calendar to alert you about recurring appointments. Get your university email forwarded to your personal email, only check your emails twice a day and deal with the ones that need to be dealt with there and then.

Time-suckers

'Time-sucker' is our term for activities that we all do instead of getting on with whatever it is we really should be doing. They tend to suck up precious time but don't offer much in return, even though you might feel as if you are doing something productive. Examples include organising your notes and papers, tidying your desk, casually browsing your university virtual learning environment, or typing up your notes.

At their worst, time-suckers are activities that we just lapse into, without thinking, and before we know it, the day has just gone, and we are no further on with our studies.

The internet is the obvious one — we can lose days watching cute puppy videos or browsing Twitter. Another time-sucker is housework. Yes, it needs doing, but is cleaning the skirting boards/weeding the garden/re-jigging the lounge/sorting out the laundry really more important than writing the essay that is due in next week? It's more likely that these are displacement activities, where you con yourself into thinking you are doing something constructive with your time, but really you are only doing them to avoid what you should *really* be doing.

Unfortunately, displacement activities don't disguise the feelings of guilt and anxiety you get from not doing what you should really be doing. You will feel much better if you *just get on with that essay*, and the more you just get on with your studying and resist your time-suckers, the easier it gets! So, identify your time-suckers and banish them, perhaps using them as rewards for when you have achieved your aims for the day, if they are really that irresistible.

These are just some ideas for time management that work for us or have worked for our students. You will develop your own strategies as time goes on. Review how you are using your time on a regular basis, get rid of time-suckers, and get organised from the outset – it will take some effort, but the pay-offs are huge.

The alternative to all this, of course, is to bumble around with no clear idea of what you should be doing, missing deadlines and not making any progress with your studies. It doesn't bear thinking about, really.

Your study environment

One of the first things you should do when you start your course (or even before) is identify a place where you can study productively. This will probably be wherever you call home (including halls of residence), but let us make it clear that this place shouldn't be your bed 😵

It's worth saying that this space should be quiet. Don't fool yourself into thinking you can study with the TV/music/kids playing in the background. When you are thinking hard, silence, white noise, or ambient sounds (including classical music – film soundtracks are great) are aids to concentration – other sounds, less so. We are confident in saying that no-one works well in a noisy environment.

You will need a desk, a chair and good lighting. Preferably, your chosen area will be somewhere where you can leave your books and papers out after a study session – it soon gets annoying having to unpack at the beginning of a session and then pack away at the end. You want a place that is ready for action at a moment's notice. This is much less likely to happen if you have to find your bag/laptop/book/a crucial piece of paper first, and then clear a space to work in.

Equip your work space with everything you need to study effectively

Avoiding distraction in the home

It's actually really hard to work effectively at home – it's strange how doing the washing up or sorting out the laundry can look really appealing next to writing a 3000-word essay! It's worth scoping out some alternative places to work for those times when you need a change of scene or working at home just isn't happening.

Below is a table of our suggestions of where you might want to work. What are the pros and cons of studying in each location for you?

	Pros	Cons
Coffee Shop		
University library		
Friend's house		

Most of your studying will inevitably be done at home, for reasons of convenience and comfort, and so these tips will help you work effectively:

- A door is useful – close it when you are working and make it clear to the rest of the household that you are working and should be disturbed only in an emergency. Likewise, at the end of your study session, closing the door behind you when you leave helps you to switch off.
- Make a flask of tea so you don't have to leave your desk to make another cup of tea, thereby leaving you at risk of being distracted.
- Take snacks with you, for the reason given above.
- Set yourself some targets for the day, so you feel that you are making progress.
- There are programmes that you can download to your computer that block access to certain sites for a set period of time – useful so you don't get distracted by social media.
- Have regular breaks but set yourself a time limit for them; 'Fifteen minutes break – I'll be back at my desk by 12:30'.
- Make sure you stretch regularly – being hunched over a laptop can give you a bad neck/back.
- Make your work space appealing – some motivational posters, plentiful desk-space, good lighting, and a supportive chair are essential.

Our best tip: treat study as if it's a job with regular hours.

7 READING FOR A PURPOSE

A student, Helene, came into our office last year in tears. Her bag was heavily laden with eight university text books which she had diligently collected from the library. Helene had input the title of her first-year assessment into the online library catalogue and the catalogue had churned out the aforementioned eight books and a couple of academic journal articles. We asked her to take a seat and to tell us what her problem was.

"I have ten days to research, plan and write a 3,000-word assignment, I have got the books from the library, but I have worked out that it will take me three weeks just to read these books, I am so stressed".

Poor Helene, she was inconsolably upset. She needed to learn some reading strategies. She had come to the right place at the right time.

In order that this chapter helps you to the full, you will need access to a stopwatch. Most mobile phones have this facility; take a moment to familiarise yourself with its function.

When you are familiar with how to use the stopwatch function on your phone, get ready to time yourself reading Passage 1.

Passage 1

University students' experiences of their first year of study has been of interest to researchers of higher education for decades. More recently, there has been a significant shift towards making higher education accessible to people from diverse backgrounds who, in previous years, might not have considered degree-level a possibility. This widening participation agenda could be considered a success, as there has been a marked increase in the number of undergraduate students from lower socio-economic groups. However, this expansion has demanded that universities provide better support to students to ensure their success, and so research into the first-year experience is essential in order to inform our understanding of what support is needed, particularly in terms of the specific support requirements of different student groups. The key themes that have emerged out of this research should be of great interest to university policy-makers and the government, as well as practitioners and researchers within higher education.

153 words

How long did this passage take you to read? One minute? Two minutes? How would you rate your comprehension of the above passage? Good? OK? Not very good?

Below is another passage to read (Passage 2). This time, only allow yourself the same time that it took you to read Passage 1. If it took you one minute, then set your timer for one minute, if it took you two minutes, then set your timer for two. There are rules here; you must read to the end of the passage and you have to read at least twice as quickly as you did the first time.

Here are some tips to help you combat the stress of this task.

Tip 1: Force your eyes to move down the page quicker than they normally do when you are reading.

Tip 2: Only read the first two sentences from every paragraph.

Tip 3: Skip over any words that are not familiar to you.

Passage 2

It is unlikely that research into factors that affect the performance of students in their first year would reveal a 'silver bullet' – one aspect of the first year of a student's degree which institutions could act upon which would radically improve the student's experience so that their withdrawal was transformed into a remote possibility. It is acknowledged that students withdraw from university for a wide variety of reasons. These reasons are complex and include both external and internal pressures.

There is some persuasive evidence to suggest that student persistence might be one of the more significant factors in terms of what makes a successful student. The more persistent a student is, the more likely they are to succeed. However, more research into the student persistence is needed to understand the role it plays for fully. How do students become persistent? What is it that makes one student more persistent than another? How can universities nurture persistence in their students?

Another factor that might play a part is the university themselves. Perhaps the choice of institution and the course is crucial. Research shows that students from the lower socio-economic groups have higher rates of withdrawal. Why might this be? Theories include a lack of

---

university-based social friendships or a reluctance to seek support. There is some research to suggest that students perform better if they live on campus. What conclusions can be drawn from this – why does living off-campus have a negative impact on student experiences?

Students' expectations of university might also contribute to their performance. Students who are the first in their family to go to university may have skewed expectations of what university is actually like and this may relate to how prepared they are when they do start their university studies.

There is also research into whether or not providing a network of support for first year students actually helps them to settle in. One significant finding of this research is the problematic conundrum that students who are in the most need of help, advice or support tend not to avail themselves of the support and as a consequence of this find the journey through university difficult. Conversely, the 'worried well' – students who are managing university life well, regularly make use of university support mechanisms and feedback that it has really helped them.

Research indicates that finances are not as big of a burden as might be supposed. Students tend to persist at university despite their financial difficulties. Some students choose (or are obliged) to take up paid work whilst they are at university but there is no evidence that working part-time whilst at university has a detrimental effect on a student's performance.

A significant number of universities class themselves as 'commuter universities', where the majority of students live at home and commute to university, as opposed to living on campus in halls of residence. There is some evidence that living on campus helps first-year students to enjoy more of a 'university experience' and perhaps make more friends more quickly, but there is no evidence that this factor alone increases either their grades at university or their persistence.

Stress and health reasons also play a large part in determining whether a student completes their degree or not. It stands to reason that a person needs good physical and mental health in order to perform well at anything, so why would this not be true of university?

568 words

Now comment in the space below what the main point of Passage 2 is:

Already you are becoming a 'quicker' reader. It is tiring to read quickly, but it is possible to read at least twice as fast as you normally read. As you get more proficient at reading quickly, you will not find the process as tiring. By using the tips listed above, and with practice, you will be able to read more quickly than you normally do. But this chapter is not called 'Fast Reading'. It is called 'Reading for a Purpose' and we would like to suggest that whilst you are at university you NEVER read without a purpose. What do we mean by this?

Bringing purpose to our reading

Purpose here means a question that you want to answer. What question do you need to answer through your reading?

For now, we will give you a question in order to practice this skill. For example, your purpose question when reading passage 2 is 'Name at least three reasons why students do not continue with their higher education studies'.

With this question in mind, set your timer and read passage two again. As soon as you have the three reasons why students do not continue with their higher education studies stop reading. How long did this passage take you to read?

The secret here is never to read without a 'purpose' or a question that you have set yourself.

If, for example, you have an assignment question in mind, then this will automatically be your purpose. Allow your eyes to skip over all other material which is not related to your assignment question.

Here is a fake assignment question and below it is another passage to read (passage 3), so that you can practise reading for a purpose.

Would you advise students to rush their academic work?

Passage 3

Tackling the writing of an essay question can be a very daunting experience for some students. Students often get 'the wrong end of the stick' when they are writing an essay. They may look at an essay title and think 'oh yes, I know something about this topic' and then begin to write everything they know about that topic.

This is not the way to answer an essay or assignment question. It is very important to read the question, read the question again, and then

---

take the time to break the question down and think about what it is actually asking. Most essay questions will demand that you focus on a particular aspect of the topic. Remember, you are only going to get marks for the words that you write if they actively go towards answering the question and the point of writing any essay question (as well as the enjoyment you may get out of writing it!) is to get marks. Just writing everything you know about the topic may mean that you fail to explore the focus of the essay question in sufficient depth.

It is quite common for students to brag about writing their essay the night before. This may well be the case - of course it is perfectly possible to write an essay in one night, even if the essay is a few thousand words long. However, it is pretty impossible to bash out a *good* essay in a few hours. What these students tend to submit is a *draft* of their essay, not a finely-honed response to the essay question. Essay writing is a craft and it takes time to perfect, both in terms of the quality and organisation of your ideas. Make sure that you leave yourself plenty of time to craft and recraft what you have written. Ideally, you should leave yourself some time to reflect on what you have written as well.

Plagiarism, where essay-writers fail to credit the sources they have used in the research and writing of their essays, is another aspect to consider when writing an essay.

The answer to the essay question above is quite obviously 'no'. And the information can be found in paragraph 3. You can allow your eyes to skip over the information in paragraphs one, two and four and slow your reading speed down a little bit when you come to paragraph 3 which contains the answer to our fake assignment question.

But, what about Helene with her eight books? How can this principle be further used to help her?

In the last three exercises you have been developing an important skill of sifting through information. You have been discarding the information which is not relevant or helpful to you. Don't forget, you are in charge of your reading; *the book is not in charge*! This principle of discarding information can be extended. You can sift through the information in 8, 10 or even 20 books in minutes if you know what you are doing.

Using contents pages

Contents pages are there for a reason. They help the reader to navigate through the book. You do not have to read every chapter of a book in order to gain the information you need for your assignment. If your assignment question asks about *crime rates in 1980* then you can confidently ignore any chapters which may talk about the *crime rate before 1980* or *social housing or crimes in 1990*. Be sure to be ruthless when you are discarding the material that you are *not* going to read. The more material you can discard, the more time you will have to spend on what really matters; reading for the purpose of your assignment.

The next practice exercise takes you through the process of discarding information. Your fake assignment question is:

What advice would you give to a new student about how to balance their learning time and family time?

The book we are suggesting for this activity is probably going to be the next book we write. Let's call it 'Making it at uni: how to supercharge your academic skills'. It's a super book, but very detailed, and in order to answer your fake question you would not need to read through the whole of the book. A lot of the material in the book would not be necessary for your fake assignment question. On the next page is a list of the chapters from the book. Cross out the chapters that you are going to 'discard'. Remember, your title is what advice would you give to a new student about how to balance their learning time and family time? Be ruthless.

Chapter 1   Supercharging your learning
Chapter 2   Developing your research skills
Chapter 3   Making useful notes
Chapter 4   Writing to learn
Chapter 5   Learning to write more academically
Chapter 6   Making time for your studies
Chapter 7   Ideas on how to be more organised
Chapter 8   Making the most of lectures
Chapter 9   Reading academic texts

We hope that your list looks something like this:

~~Chapter 1   Supercharging your learning~~
~~Chapter 2   Developing your research skills~~
~~Chapter 3   Making useful notes~~
~~Chapter 4   Writing to learn~~
~~Chapter 5   Learning to write more academically~~
Chapter 6   Making time for your studies
~~Chapter 7   Ideas on how to be more organised~~
~~Chapter 8   Making the most of lectures~~
~~Chapter 9   Reading academic texts~~

The only chapter which is relevant to our fake assignment title of *'What advice would you give to a new student about how to balance their learning time and family time?'* is the chapter on 'Making time for your studies'.

Using an index

A book index is an *alphabetized list of words and phrases showing the page numbers on which writing on the particular subject can be found.* The index is typically placed at the end of a book. An index can be found in most text books. If the information that you are searching for is not immediately evident from the list of chapters at the front of the book, then you may wish to narrow down your search a bit and have a look at the index. The index will list every place in the book where your search term is mentioned. An index can be extremely useful, but beware; they can also be a huge waste of your valuable research time. Many a time have we looked in an index only to be directed to pages and pages of writing which has nothing to do with what we need for our work. So be careful; use the index of a book with caution and don't rush in thinking that every page listed in the index under the word or phrase you are looking for is valuable information for your assignment.

Poor Helene carrying around eight books

Did Helene have to carry around these eight books? No, of course not. If she had applied the reading strategies above, then she could have photocopied or scanned the sections which were relevant to her work and left the book in the library for some other unsuspecting student to carry home and cry over. Sometimes, we tend to make the tasks in front of us into mountains which seem too difficult to climb. Helene was quite right in her observation that she would not be able to read eight books in time to plan and write her assignment. But she had created this task for herself! No one had asked her to 'read' eight books.

We looked at her assignment question and sifting through the chapters of the books which we thought were going to be relevant to her assignment. We skimmed through the chapters to make sure that they were worth photocopying and then put post-it notes inside the books to remind Helene which chapters she needed to photocopy. She was going to check in with us the next day.

She visited our office the following day and the feeling of overwhelming stress had been lifted. She now had a reading 'plan'. She admitted that over the past couple of days that she had actually learned to READ.

"No, Helene, you knew how to read, you just needed to learn how to read for a purpose."

8 WRITING

There are hundreds of books out there that go on and on and on about how to write good essays at university. This amazes us, because there is no 'right' way of writing essays. But, still, if authors feel that it is a good idea to take students through step by step on how to write a good university essay then good luck to them. And good luck to the unsuspecting students who sit down to read them.

You are obviously (quite) a competent writer, otherwise you wouldn't be thinking of going to university. But, being a competent writer is not all that is needed at university. It is our hope in this chapter that we can show you a few tricks of the trade which you can apply to your already competent writing, so that you manage to impress your lecturer when they come to mark your assignment.

Writing at university will be a whole new ballgame

It is recommended that you spend a couple of hours working through and practising the material in this chapter in order to get the hang of three basic techniques. Don't skip over things in this chapter, read it very carefully. You may want to read this 'Writing' chapter alongside the chapter on 'Referencing'. Make your own practice exercises using any book that you have to hand. All of the words written within a book can have the three techniques in this chapter applied to them. There will be no lack of practice material.

First of all, note down in the box below the types of writing you have done in the past. For example, reports for college, letters to grandmother, article for school magazine, etc.

Some of this writing will be along the same lines as that required at university, for example an A Level essay on the Second World War. Then again, some of the writing that you have done in the past will bear no relevance to the writing that is required of you at university, for example a text message to your girlfriend or boyfriend.

What are the differences between these types of writing? Writing that is required at university is formal and well-structured and displays a good use of language and grammar. It is often thematic and written in order to answer a question. It is divided into paragraphs and cohesive sentences. And it is always evidenced.

The writing that is required of you at university will always need to be evidenced. This simply means that you will not be able to sit down and write about ideas that have popped into your head. You will have to have researched what other authors are writing about your topic before you begin to write. In other words, you will have to read, before you begin your writing (see the chapter on Reading for a Purpose). If you are sure of the information that you are going to use from your reading, then you can begin to write. Remember, you are not going to get any marks for your writing unless it answers the question. Only the other day Jake came into our office for some assignment feedback. His question was 'What are the problems facing the legal system today?' Jake had written, beautifully, 3,000 words of very eloquent writing and he was confident when he handed in the essay. However, Jake received a fail mark for his writing. Why do you think this was? Jake had not answered the question. He had written four or five sentences outlining the problems facing the legal system then he had written 2,800 words outlining very well-thought-out and well-written *solutions* to these problems. He had not answered the question. The moral of Jake's story is: keep focused on the question. Whenever you feel that you are tempted to write 'extra' information which sounds good and flows well in your essay, but doesn't go towards answering the question, then scrap it. You won't get any marks for it.

Very Important Tip: Answer the question!

The next couple of things we want to talk about are not really tips, they are techniques. One student even called them 'cheats'. But this is not cheating. This is learning the techniques that you can apply to your writing over and over again. But if you want to think of it as cheating, then that's fine - we do agree that knowing how to use these techniques properly will make your life easier.

We have already stated in this chapter that the writing which is required of you at university must be evidenced. We are going to show you three ways here of showing your lecturer that you have 'evidenced' your writing, and what's more that you know what you are talking about. It is really important that you read this chapter alongside the chapter on referencing. Writing and referencing are inextricably linked at university - one does not exist without the other. So a good place to start when writing your first essays at university is to focus on how you use quotations, summarising ideas from longer books, and paraphrasing short extracts.

Technique 1: using quotations

'Using quotations' in this book comes with a health warning. Too many quotations in your work can make you appear lazy, disengaged and unable to write. So please use quotations very sparingly. Use them like you would a picture illustration. Use them when absolutely nothing else will do, when you need to use the exact words of the author and no other words will be able to back up your point. Warning over.

The rules surrounding how to punctuate quotations are a bit complicated and to be honest, a bit woolly at times, so we are going to present two rules on punctuating quotations which you will find useful.

This is the first rule. If the text that you wish to use for your quotation is short (i.e. two lines or fewer) then your quotation needs to be placed within your writing and put into quotation marks.

This is an example of how you would embed a shorter quote in your sentence in an essay:

We can observe that many authors talk about reading and writing; "There are hundreds of books out there that go on and on and on about how to write good essays at university" (Bartholomew and Withers, 2018, px). But our job is to sift through the information that we don't need in order to get to the information that we do need.

This is the second rule: if the text that you wish to use for your quotation is longer than two lines, then you will need to indent your quotation:

We can observe that many authors talk about reading and writing:

"There are hundreds of books out there that go on and on and on about how to write good essays at university. This amazes us as there is no 'right' way of writing essays at university. But, still, if authors feel that it is a good idea to take students through step by step on how to write a good university essay then good luck to them" (Bartholomew and Withers, 2018 p.3).

But our job is to sift through the information that we don't need in order to get to the information that we do need.

IMPORTANT: We get asked this question over and over again: 'Do I have to reference a quotation?' Yes! Always say where you got your quotation from (this is called an in-text citation - more on this in our chapter on referencing). When referencing a quotation, it is also a good idea to put in the page number of where you have taken the quotation from. But do not be tempted to include the name of the book or journal article; just include the surname/s of the author/s, year of publication and page number. Put this information in brackets after the quotation.

Technique 2: summarising

If we were to ask you what happened in your favourite TV programme last night, would you be able to do it? In fact, write in the box below what did happen:

Very good. Thank you. That will save us time watching it on catch-up! You have illustrated above that you are a summary writing expert! You can summarise the on-screen 30 minutes of events of your favourite TV programme in less than 5 minutes. And we can read about it in one minute. We are all naturally very good at summarising things. If someone asks you what you did at the weekend, you don't go through every minute detail talking about all the food you ate, the weather, if your dog was well behaved and the time the postman knocked on your door. You simply relay the most important or relevant events to the person who has enquired: 'Yes, I had a lovely weekend, I visited London with my family, and it was super'.

A summary of a passage is a shortened, condensed version which is written in your own words. A summary talks only about the main points of a passage and misses out all of the details. The original passage could be 1,000 words long and your summary may only be 100 words. There is no exact science around summary-writing word counts but they are always shorter. A summary is always considerably shorter than the original passage.

The main thing to remember when summarising a piece of writing from another source is the importance of *your understanding* of its ideas. You must make sure that you thoroughly understand the text before you begin to summarise it. The reason that we are so good at summarising the last episode of our favourite TV programme or the time we spent at the weekend is that we thoroughly understood what was going on. Do not attempt to summarise any passage without understanding what is being spoken about.

A good way of writing a summary is to follow these steps:

1. Read the passage and thoroughly understand what is said.

2. Highlight the important bits with a highlighter pen

3. Note down these highlighted sections in your notebook. For now, you can use the words of the author, or start using your own words if you prefer. A word of caution here though – make sure that you are not changing the meaning of what the author said.

4. Re-read your own notes which you took from the original passage. Close your note book and begin writing your summary in your essay. Try to use your own words and not those used directly by the author of the original passage.

IMPORTANT: We get asked this question over and over again: 'Do I have to reference a summary?' Yes! Follow the same rule that we explained above for referencing a quotation: include the surname/s of the author/s, year of publication. Put this information in brackets after the summary. Page numbers are not needed when summarising as the information included in a summary generally can't be found on a specific page, as summaries reflect your overall understanding and re-stating of the author's argument.

Technique 3: paraphrasing

A paraphrase is another way of using someone else's ideas in your own writing. It is another way of evidencing what you have written. It is a legitimate way of transferring information from your source (that book you got out of the library yesterday) to your work (the essay that is due in next Monday). In a paraphrase, you will rephrase or rewrite the original text in different words without changing the original meaning.

So, the following *original* sentence, written by Bloggs in 2018:

John walked into the room, sat on the chair and then started talking to Margaret.

can be paraphrased as:

John began speaking to Margaret after he had entered the room and was seated (Bloggs, 2018).

Note here that we have not changed the meaning of the sentence. The same story exists; the story about John and Margaret talking after John has come into the room and sat down. But the words have changed. Two techniques have been used here to convert the original into a paraphrase; the use of synonyms (words that have the same meaning) and the use of jig-sawing phrases (moving the parts of the sentence around).

These synonyms have been used:

Original word/phrase	Replaced by synonym
walked	entered
talking	speaking
sat on a chair	was seated

Note that some words have stayed the same. The word 'room', for example, is very difficult to find a synonym for; it certainly wouldn't be a good idea to replace the word 'room' for the phrase 'part of a building'.

Try hovering your cursor over a word that you have written in a Microsoft Word document. Right click your mouse on the word and, from the menu that pops up, select 'Synonyms' to look up the programme's suggestions for alternative words - it's a really useful tool. But make sure you use your common sense: make sure your sentence still makes sense and reads well after you have replaced the original words with synonyms.

Jig-sawing phrases

Because of the characteristics of the English language, it is possible for us to change the order of words in a sentence without changing the meaning of the sentence. Note that in our example sentence we have the word 'talking' towards the end of the sentence, but in our paraphrased version this has moved toward the beginning of the sentence. But the meaning of the sentence has not changed, nor has the order of events! This is because we have added the word *after* in our paraphrase. *After* here is what is known in the grammar trade (we won't bore you too much) as a *connective preposition*; here are a few more connective prepositions which you may want to use:

> *as   before   when   while   as soon as   until*

Tip: Search on the internet for a few more to add to this list, and then refer to it for ideas when you are writing your own paraphrases.

IMPORTANT: We get asked this question over and over again: 'Do I have to reference a paraphrase?' Yes! Just like when quoting and summarising, you should always reference paraphrased information by including an in-text citation. Here is another tip for linking your quotation, summary or paraphrase into your writing.

Words which link what you have already said in your writing to the quotation, summary or paraphrase are called reporting words. Here are some useful reporting words that you could use when quoting, summarising or paraphrasing. See if you can think of any more (there are lots of words which you can use):

reported
stated
mentioned
maintained
insisted
declared
wrote
pointed out

Understanding the few bits of advice we have explained in this chapter will be the first step in understanding what it means to write in an academic style. There is no quick fix to becoming a good writer at university. The answer lies in giving yourself time, space and practice. Lots and lots of practice. The best advice we can give you is to have a go. Be brave and believe in yourself as a writer. Use the techniques listed in this chapter and you will be on your way to accomplishing great things.

When you have done a piece of writing for university and handed it in, your writing will be marked. This essay or assignment may make the grade or not: it may pass, or it may fail. The most important thing to gain from your writing journey at university is to learn from your successes and your mistakes. Lecturers are required to give you feedback on your writing. They are required to communicate with you what they thought was good and what they thought was not so good about your assignment.

In our experience as lecturers, the biggest error that students make is not the mistakes that they make in their writing, but the mistakes they make in not listening to or reading their feedback from their lecturer. Your writing experience at university is a learning experience. Each piece of writing you submit should be a little bit better than the last. You should be able to listen to and understand the feedback from the lecturer who has marked your work. You should then be able to apply this understanding to your next piece of work. Lecturers are there to help you to improve; it is in their interest that you get better, so please make sure that you arrange the necessary appointments to talk about your work with your lecturing staff.

9 REFERENCING

There is one word that strikes fear into the hearts of students in their first semester.

Lecturers denounce it.

The word is spoken in hushed tones. Students become petrified of committing the *offence*.

The word is…plagiarism.

In this chapter, we will describe and explain referencing. Referencing accurately will make sure you don't inadvertently plagiarise.

A journey through referencing

There are three stages that students seem to progress through when it comes to the arcane skill of referencing.

The first stage is blissful ignorance, where you don't even know that it exists. A very small number of misguided or misinformed students linger in this group for a little longer than is good for them. They don't realise that there are rules about how you use other people's ideas when writing academically. However, just by reading the last few paragraphs, you are no longer at this stage – well done!

Stage two is the 'not-quite-there-yet' stage. You know you have to reference, as your lecturers mention it in lectures. You will have had a go at it in your first assignments, but you might be making a few errors. Some of you might be offered the chance to take a module that focuses on your academic skills. This is great - you can ask questions and get feedback on your referencing. All universities will offer referencing workshops, which again are well worth attending. At the very least, you must check out your library/department's referencing guide (look on your university website or ask a librarian: every university librarian will be able to point you in the right direction).

Students in the third and final stage have absolutely nailed referencing. You will have an appreciation of why we do it and why it's important. You are complimented on the accuracy of your referencing, and you take pride in presenting a beautifully organised reference list in which all the commas are in the right place, authors' names are spelled correctly, and the bits that need to be *italicised* or in **bold** are indeed *italicised* or in **bold** *(never both at the same time, though)*.

The recipe for referencing success is pretty simple:

- Keep clear records of what you read (author, title, page numbers, etc.)

- Have an eye for detail, following the referencing instructions to the letter.

- Make time to create your reference list as you go along, so you don't run out of time to do it properly.

- Keep a well-thumbed Harvard referencing manual at your side when writing.

There is no reason why every student shouldn't be in the last group by the end of their first semester. With this handy guide, you can make sure that you are.

So, why do we reference?

Contrary to most people's expectations, we don't reference solely to avoid charges of plagiarism (which means copying someone else's ideas and words and not giving them credit). The truth is a little more interesting, and also illustrates the importance of referencing. Wait for it...

We reference to show our readers the breadth and depth of our reading. The quality of the sources we use, and how we present them in our writing, has a direct impact on the quality of our writing.

This is because the name of the game when studying at university is your engagement with the academic conversations in your discipline. As an undergraduate student, your role is to listen to all of the debates, theories etc. and then explain them to the readers of your essays to show your understanding of them. By presenting and then discussing the ideas from your reading in your essays, you are showing your reader just how extensive your reading is, as well as how well you have understood what you have read.

OK, so it's important – how do I do it?

The first thing to note is that this is a general guide, and you should find out what referencing system your subject and your department uses. The following is just for illustrative purposes and is based on the most widely-used system, Harvard-style referencing. Some subjects (Law, History, the Arts) are likely to use a quite different system. One of your jobs as a student is to ensure that you find this stuff out – don't wait to be told!

There are two parts to referencing:

Including an in-text citation, which can use the name-date system e.g. (Jones, 2018) or a superscript[5] and footnote.
Including a reference list at the end of the text. The sources are arranged in alphabetical order, by surname.

The in-text citation draws the reader's attention to the fact that you have brought in someone else's words and ideas (see the Writing chapter for how and why you do this).

---

[5] This is a footnote and the small number is called a superscript.

The reference list then gives the full details of the source, so that the reader, should they want to, could locate and read the source for themselves. Lecturers will most definitely look at your reference list, as they can see, briefly, what you have chosen to read and cite in your writing. It is fair to say that lecturers will expect you to master the skill, and there is very little tolerance for sloppy referencing, especially once you get into your second year and beyond. First years are obviously still learning, so the penalties are not so harsh, but there is an expectation that some effort will be put into it, even if some aspects are not yet fully understood. It's pretty impossible for a poorly referenced piece of work to be given the highest marks (exceptions might be reflective pieces of writing, say in Education or in the Arts), and in our experience if a student can reference well, the rest of their work is likely to be of good quality, and vice versa.

What does a reference list look like?

Grab any academic text that you have to hand (any textbook would do), and glance down the reference list. You will see that the details of each text are given in a very particular fashion. Different types of texts (genres) are laid out differently. This is one of the most important things to remember – that you have to give different information in the reference list depending on what type of text you are providing the reference for.

Try to work out what type of text is represented by each reference and match them in the table on the next page (note the reference system used here is Harvard):

Text types to match:

- Printed book
- Chapter of an edited book
- Electronic journal article
- Online newspaper

Text type	What the reference will look like in reference list
	Shirazi, T. (2010) 'Successful teaching placements in secondary schools: achieving QTS practical handbooks', *European Journal of Teacher Education*, 33(3), pp. 323–326. doi: 10.1080/02619761003602246.
	Roberts, D. and Ackerman, S. (2013) 'US draft resolution allows Obama 90 days for military action against Syria', *The Guardian*, 4 September. Available at: http://www.theguardian.com/world/2013/sep/04/syria-strikes-draft-resolution-90-days (Accessed: 9 September 2015).
	Bell, J. (2014) *Doing your research project*. Maidenhead: Open University Press.
	Franklin, A.W. (2012) 'Management of the problem', in Smith, S.M. (ed.) *The maltreatment of children*. Lancaster: MTP, pp. 83–95.

You can use the examples above as templates to practise how to reference a book, newspaper article, journal article or chapter of an edited book. When you are at university, though, you must make sure you are clear about what the referencing system for your course/module looks like and follow those rules. The differences are likely to be very, very small (maybe we have used a full stop in the (ed.) part, but your referencing system doesn't) but you should follow your course's system nonetheless.

Reference management systems

There are a few free citation tools – neilstoolbox.com and citethisforme.com are free online citation generators, and are pretty good, although they are only as good as the information you put in – you still need to ensure your spelling is accurate and you include capital letters where needed. The software won't put these in for you. These systems will arrange the information into roughly the right order, but make sure you check the final reference and make any changes needed so that it matches your course/module's system. Microsoft Word has a handy feature which will alphabetise your reference list for you – highlight your reference list and then click on the little icon that says *A-Z* with a downward-facing arrow.

Top Tips

Watch the spelling of people's names and check their gender – there is nothing more annoying than someone repeatedly referring to an author as 'he' when she is in fact a 'she'.

Reference as you go along – there is nothing more painful than completing an essay and then, exhausted and fed up, having to hunt down the texts you used so you can reference them.

Increase the font size when writing your reference list – it makes it easier to check the punctuation is in the right place. Just remember to reduce the font size when you are finished.

Commonly-held referencing misconceptions

A bibliography and a reference list are not the same, as people sometimes think. A reference list will list all of the texts referred to in the essay, whereas a bibliography lists all of the texts used in the writing of a document, even if they were not directly cited. So, you will generally find bibliographies in academic books rather than in student essays.

Referencing fun facts

- There are over 7000 referencing styles – do you know which style your subject uses?

- Referencing styles are named after people and institutions: Harvard after Harvard University; MLA was designed by the Modern Language Association: American Psychological Association designed the APA system.

Sneaky Cheats!

If your reading list is presented as a reference list (say in a module guide), cut and paste the references for the sources you have used into your essay!

10 ENDINGS (AND NEW BEGINNINGS)

If you have worked your way through this book then you should be well equipped to face the rigours of higher education. You should have learned some lessons about how to settle in at university and made some steps towards making friends. A few of these friends will stay with you for life, so take plenty of pictures to jog your memory in years to come!

You will have realised that all scary things are not bad and even though you were nervous about entering your first lecture theatre, you were surrounded by lots of people in the same situation as you. And you survived!

You will have learned a little bit about how important it is to take care of your physical and mental health and we hope that you develop your own strategies to Keep Calm and Carry On. Please share any tips and advice with our readers on our blog. Also, let us know if you've developed any nutritious, cheap recipes so that we can pass them on to other new students next year.

We hope that you have at least thought about getting more organised and the benefits that this will bring you in the long term. Organisation may slip from time to time but providing you know how to get back on track, you'll be fine. There will soon come a time when you won't be relying on the charts and tables in this book and you will know your timetable and where you're supposed to be off by heart. But use the scribbles you have made in this book for as long as you need to.

You will have read about the importance of staying on track with your money and how not to get into bad debt. You have been guided through how to budget for all of your student essentials and what not to waste your money on. You can have fun on a budget. A student loan is an investment, an investment in you and your future. An investment into what you want to become – a better you!

Finally, you should have gained a little insight into the reading, writing and referencing conventions at university. There is a lot more to be said about this but now is not the time for us to overburden you. Now is the time for you to feel confident in yourself and to perform to the very best of your ability.

We hope that the information in the chapters on reading, writing and referencing has given you an appetite to find out more. Most universities have excellent websites where you should be able to learn more about the conventions of your institution and more about what is expected of you when you research and write. Never forget that you *can* do it. You can research and you *can* write essays. But it takes time and practice. Listen very carefully to the feedback from your tutors and try to take a step forward in every new assignment.

Please feel free to share your experiences with us at **makingitatuni.wordpress.com** or **@makingitatuni**. In reading the postings and tweets there you will realise that you are not alone. There are thousands of new students who, just like you, are taking their first steps into the unknown. Our aim in this book is to make the climate of university a little warmer and enable you to enter with confidence. Be brave and enjoy!

Sally and Jodi

P.S. As you make your way through your first few months as an undergraduate, why not take part in our 'first-year bingo' game, which you will find on the next page? When you've ticked them all off, you will know you have had a true student experience!

BONUS CHAPTER: FIRST YEAR BINGO

Nobody speaks in a seminar	Your computer loses your work (genuinely)	Someone mistakes a lecturer for a student	You miss a lecture because you have to finish an assignment due in that day	A piece of reading is completely impenetrable
A topic you are struggling with suddenly makes sense	You are so engrossed in some reading you miss your train/bus stop	It kicks off in a lecture because someone is talking and annoying someone sitting nearby	A fellow student falls asleep in a lecture	Your lecturer has a hole in their jumper or wears an 'interesting' scarf
You do all the work in a group task	You call your lecturer 'miss' or 'sir' by accident	You question why you are doing this to yourself	Getting your first grades back	First lecture!
Insert your own milestone here	Handing in your first assignments	Insert your own milestone here	Getting your student ID – discounts galore!	Working in the library at midnight

REFERENCES

BBC (2017) *Meet some of the UK's oldest university students*. Available at: http://www.bbc.co.uk/news/education-41573213. (Accessed 18 December 2018).

HESA (2019) *Who's studying in HE*. Available at: https://www.hesa.ac.uk/data-and-analysis/students/whos-in-he. (Accessed 30 March 2019).

Lewis, M. (2018) *Student Loans Mythbusting*. Available at: https://www.moneysavingexpert.com/students/student-loans-tuition-fees-changes/. (Accessed 18 December 2018).

APPENDIX

This handy table explains the meaning of some of the terms that are used a lot at university. There is space at the end for you to add any new words you come across that aren't already mentioned.

Academic year	The academic year runs from September to August. Academic years are normally divided into semesters. Add here the dates of your semesters so you know when your lectures are due to start and end. Your university website might be a good place to start to look for this information.
Accredited degree	An accredited degree that meets specific educational standards which have been set by the accreditation body. Choosing an accredited degree means that employers will recognise the 'worthiness' of your qualification. What is the full title of the qualification you are studying at university?
Alumni	Alumni are former graduates of the university, students who have studied at the university before you. You may want to spend a bit of time researching if there are any noteworthy people who attended your university before you. Note down their names here:

BA, BEng, BSc	Bachelor of Arts degree, Bachelor of Engineering, Bachelor of Science. Which type of degree are you studying?
Campus	The campus is the buildings and grounds of the university. Sometimes campuses can be spread over several different locations. Make sure that you are in possession of a map of your campus so that you know where things are. Explore the campus in your first few weeks.
Careers and enterprise	There is normally a place within universities where you can go to get free advice on gaining work experience and opportunities to network with employers and alumni. There may even be information on starting your own business, help with applications, interviews, part time work, internships, graduate schemes and further study. Mark on your map where your careers and enterprise services are located and note down in your diary a time to pass by there and see what is on offer.
Course representatives	A course rep is someone who seeks out student views and represents these views in some form of staff/ student liaison committee. You may be invited to be a course rep; why not? Have a go. What have you got to lose?
Credits	Often, each unit of study (normally a module) carries credits. You will have to pass a minimum number of credits in order to proceed in your course, e.g. to move from your first year of study to your second. Check in your university information what these credits are and how you might have to achieve them.
Disability and dyslexia service	If you are a student with a registered disability, then you should seek out the help that you are entitled to from your university. Go along to the place where the help is offered at your university and ask some questions.
Extenuating Circumstances	Extenuating Circumstances may be called something different in your university but, essentially, they are 'circumstances which are

	outside the student's control which may have a negative impact on the student's ability to complete an assessment'. You may find yourself in a situation which is unavoidable and not your fault around the time of assessment deadlines, which will prevent you from handing in your assessment. There will be some way for you to communicate this to the university and a procedure which you can follow in order that you are given a fair chance. What this 'fair chance' means depends on your university. Write down here the rules around extenuating circumstances in your institution:
Employability	Employability describes work readiness – how ready someone is for work. Universities are measured and accredited on how good their students' employability is. As a consequence of this many universities have put a lot of money into initiatives which will help you to be more employable. Find out what these initiatives are and list some of them below.
Enrolment	Enrolment is the process of officially registering with the university. This is compulsory. It proves that you are committed to being a student for the duration of your course. Take this decision seriously and for the right reasons. Don't enrol at university just because your friends are doing it or because you have nothing else to do with your life. Enrol because you want to go on the journey that university will present you with, because you want to have a fuller, better-qualified next stage of your life.
Faculty	A faculty is a division of a university. Your course is within a faculty. In which faculty is your course?

Formative assessment	Formative assessment is any assessment where the grade you are given (if you are given one at all) does not count towards your final grade in the module. The purpose of these assessments is for you to 'have a go' and to receive feedback on your work in order that when you do the 'summative' assessment (see below) you are better prepared.
Foundation programmes	Foundation programmes are designed to prepare students for further undergraduate study.
Halls of residence	Halls of residence are normally university-owned accommodation blocks for students. These halls will be managed by the accommodation services team. Make sure here that you know the contact details of any services you might need if you are staying in halls of residence:
HE	HE stands for higher education. A period of study at degree level or higher. Normally university!
Lecture	A talk delivered by a member of teaching staff. Do you know where all of your lectures will be held and at what times you are expected to be there?
Module	A module is normally a unit of study made up of several hours of lectures. Normally you will have some choice in the modules that you are studying in any given semester. Note down here the modules you are studying this semester:
Module leader	Your module leader is an important point of contact regarding queries relating to your module.
Module registration	Module registration is the process of selecting the modules which you are going to study over the semester. You will not be able to study these modules until you have registered on them. Make sure you have chosen the appropriate modules for your route of study. There should be someone

	to help you with this process if you need it. Who are these people at your university?
NUS	The NUS is the National Union of Students. This is an organisation of students whose job it is to advise and support the student body.
Personal tutor	Your personal tutor is someone who can help you to develop as a student at university. Make sure that you are aware of how to make an appointment with your PT. What is your PT's name? Write their name and office number here:
Plagiarism	Plagiarism is the act of using someone else's work so that the reader may assume that it is your own work. Sometimes students plagiarise unintentionally, which is a shame. Make sure you know the rules and consequences around plagiarism at your university. Refer to our chapter on referencing for more information on how to avoid plagiarism.
Reading list	A reading list is a list of books and other sources which your lecturer recommends that you read in order to tackle your assessment.
Semester	'Semester' is an American word which we have adopted for use in Britain. It means a term of study. Some universities have two semesters per year, others have three.
Student finance	Student finance represents the body which is supplying you with the money to pay for your degree. Write here the contact email and telephone number for student finance and also any questions that you may have e.g. When will I get my payment for semester two? There is usually someone who can liaise with your student finance body at your university. Who is this person?
Student ID number	All students are given a student ID number on enrolling at a university. This is your unique number which you will be required to quote many

	times over the course of your study. Make sure you know it and memorise it. Write down your student ID number here:
Student support	All universities have places where students can go to find support with a whole range of issues, from help with writing an essay to mental health and hardship problems. Where is your student support based? Write here some of the important contacts in student support:
Summative assessment	Summative assessment is any assessment where the grade you are given counts towards the final grade in the module. You should be given feedback on this work and the reasons why you passed or failed the assessment. It is important that you understand the feedback; if you don't, ask your lecturer for an appointment in order to explain the feedback to you.
Add your own words and definitions below:	

The next few pages are blank so you can make a note of any key information you need to remember.

NOTES

NOTES

NOTES

NOTES

NOTES

ABOUT THE AUTHORS

Sally Bartholomew has been working in higher education for over twenty years. She is currently working at the University of Wolverhampton in the West Midlands. She is a Principal Lecturer and Head of Student Experience and Academic Skills for the Faculty of Social Sciences. She holds a Master's degree in Applied Linguistics and a diploma in the teaching of students with Specific Learning Difficulties (SpLD) as well as the Trinity Diploma in the Teaching of English as a Foreign Language; she is a Senior Fellow of the Higher Education Academy. She is currently studying for her PhD which focuses on measuring the added value of one-to-one academic assistance for mainstream students in higher education. She is married and has four children, three of whom have attended or are attending university. Her fourth child, Lily, is at the time of writing 6 years old. We are sure that this book, as well as lots of 'lessons from Mum', will be on Lily's pre-university reading list in years to come!

Jodi Withers has worked for the University of Wolverhampton in the Faculty of Social Sciences since 2015, initially as a lecturer in academic skills but more recently as course co-ordinator of the Faculty's foundation year, which prepares students for the rigours of degree-level study. She also leads a first-year module in academic skills and is a Fellow of the Higher Education Academy. Her first degree is in English, and she is a trained teacher of adult literacy with a specialism in supporting students who are dyslexic. She has published research on student writing practices, one of her professional interests. She is currently studying for a PhD at the University of Leicester, exploring an entirely different passion: the psychology of how people think and feel about money. She has (to date) worked and/or studied at six different universities. She lives in Wolverhampton with her partner and their grumpy but adorable dog, a Westie called Gizmo.

Printed in Poland
by Amazon Fulfillment
Poland Sp. z o.o., Wrocław